AF579263

The Mighty Marathon

Volume 2

by Will Cramer

I dedicate this book to Shatiera Portee,
who loves ketchup flavored potato
chips. She is a friend that
will always inspire you
to think outside
the box.

The Mighty Marathon Volume 2

Introduction

Erik Weihenmayer climbed Mt. Everest May 25 2001. It's elevation is around 29,032 feet and is said to be the highest mountain on Earth. He also climbed the highest point in each continent starting with Denali 20,320 feet high, Kilimanjaro 19,341 feet high, Aconcagua 22,841 feet high, Vinson Massif 16,050 feet high, Elbrus 18,510 feet high, Kosciuszko 7,310 feet high, Carstensz Pyramid 16,023 feet high.

It sounds pretty amazing for an average man, but there is a piece of the puzzle you're missing. Erik is blind.

Yes, and I keep his picture above the washer machine every time I have to face my laundry. If he can do all that blind, then I can do the laundry.

Maybe now you're thinking of the challenges you face, maybe motivation, maybe just starting something, maybe just losing weight, maybe just trying to eat healthy, be a better runner or improve your life in some way.

Running for me is not about completing a half-marathon, running is about the change, the challenges, and the choices that need to take place in my life to cross the finish line.

Learning to overcome these challenges I face as a runner has improved my ability to plan, stay focused, stay motivated, seek out different resources to reinvent my life, and my running potential.

The Mighty Marathon volume 2 edition talks about the challenges you face in life as you run.

So what pops into your head when you think of challenges?

To simply put it, challenges are an invitation to overcome whatever is holding you back.

If you are stuck and can't get past your challenges this book is for you.

It talks about: * Motivation * Staying focused * Beginning * Staying healthy *Being flexible.

If you want to improve your running times and learn more about running, this book is for you.

It talks about: * Running techniques * Boosting your time naturally * Running Equipment.

If you want to avoid the pitfalls in running this book is for you.

It talks about: * When to change your running shoes * Leg Cramps * Hitting the wall * Not drinking enough fluids.

TABLE OF CONTENTS

Chapter 1

I was 20 feet from the finish line as I took my cell phone off of my waist. My body was soaked in sweat, my legs were shaking. I was trying to think of something inspiring to help me get to the finish line when an old lady half my size passed me up. I had nothing left, I was just being pulled across the finish line with her breeze.

While I crossed the finish line I pushed my under armour app to stop my time but my cell phone data was being throttled down and it took a minute to stop. I finished 13.1 miles in an hour and fifty eight minutes. Even though it was not a fast time, it was my time, and it showed me that I was making progress.

It was in November in Norfolk, Va. and it was my last official run for the season. While I was walking over to get something to eat I ran into Myra and Larry. I saw them at the starting line but lost them half way through. I asked where Courtney and Morgan were at, and they said follow us, they are over here. We sat at a huge table and laughed about everything. One by one we shared with each other the challenges we faced during the year. I started off first sharing my challenges.

There are a lot of challenges I face running all year around. A few of them are running at night, the cold weather, and eating late. Especially from November to March. I don't want to say I get scared in the dark, but I do. The night brings a lot of things out, especially when there are no street lights. The blinking lights hanging all over my body makes me feel like a living target. The only good thing about running in the dark is that it makes you forget about the cold weather.

Myra told me that one of her challenges is finding the right outfit to wear. Myra is a girly girl. She is thin with short brown hair, always wearing the latest styles. She designs clothes for an overseas company.

Larry, her boyfriend, said that his greatest challenge is avoiding the vending machines at work and the car dealers breakfast buffets. Larry has been the top car salesman at the dealership for the past 10 years. We have been friends since high school.

Courtney said that her greatest challenge was spending too much money buying clothes online and trying to get in a workout with all her kids. She is a trainer at the local gym here. I have never seen someone find so many uses for the Apple Watch but she is in touch with her clients all day long. We all have our own challenges and it's nice to laugh about them sometimes.

Morgan shared her challenges, she said just trying to find out where we are running is a challenge. She said she feels like she is out of the loop sometimes. Her dogs take up most of her time and she has a hard time finding someone to watch them while she runs.

What are your challenges? Maybe you work out by yourself and find it hard to be motivated. Maybe you look at where you want to be and feel that it's impossible to get where you want to go. You're not the only one that feels that way. You can make a difference in your life if you choose to move forward no matter what challenges you face.

Joan of Arc was just a peasant farm girl 17 years old, no horse, no armor, no experience fighting, no sword, and no army to lead. She convinced Prince Charles of Valois to allow her to lead a French army to free the city of Orleans from England.

How insane does that sound, she had no resume, no degree in combat, no license to carry a weapon, and yet she led the French army to victory at Orleans in 1429, and ended the Hundred Years War between England and France.

The power of one is strong, don't think you are alone, and don't think what you do doesn't matter, it does matter. We are going to talk about the challenges we face each day all the way through this book and how we can overcome them together.

We usually run all year around but we take a break in December for a few weeks to regroup. Plus someone has to hang up the Christmas lights, eat all the food, and sing Christmas Carols. This is the time we get together at the Brewery to grab some food and talk about the races that we want to run next year.

We sat at a huge table with flyers, running schedules, motels, places of interest to visit, and a list of new products we want to try for the upcoming year. From a distance it looks like we are planning a heist.

I do feel like a gangster though, because I am planning to heist my entire body for the upcoming year. No excuses, no quitting, no changing my mind, at this point I am all in, and if I fall, I just get up. I figure out what I need to do to move forward.

You may be thinking, is this necessary, absolutely.

The girls need to pick the motels 'cuz that's just the way it is, and I have to say it, the girls run the show, they are highly organized. I don't have a problem with that. Neither does Larry. I usually do everything on the fly but the girls make it so easy.

After coming up with the year's running plan we talk about times to meet during the winter months to practice our runs.

Everyone loves to meet at Larry's Dealership to run.

The girls like the huge bathrooms, and to be honest they sit in there and talk for a while.

Larry usually takes me for a quick test drive to blow off a few minutes. He makes me feel like I am back in high school. Riding in the sports car with the windows down takes me back a few.

While Larry was giving me the low down on the sports car, I was thinking about how to keep up with Myra on our run tonight. What does she say to herself before a run that drives that little body past all of us like we are standing still.

I'm going to ask her tonight after the run. I hope she is straight up with me and gives me her secret. It's always good to listen to others and see if what works for them may work for you. I have learned a lot from others over the years, and a lot of it has improved my running times.

Just as I finished that thought we pulled into the dealership and the girls were outside waiting for us to join them. I got out of the car with Larry and we started our run. It was a 10 mile run. About 4 miles into the run Myra took off, I was keeping up for a while but the pace was so fast I had to fall back. Courtney pulled up beside me laughing. She said no one can keep up with her 'cuz she is on a mission.

Larry passed me up and soon we were on our 7 mile. I turned around to see where Morgan was and I noticed that another girl was running with us. I have heard of people crashing a wedding party. There would be cool, delicious food, cheering, dancing, and singing going on, but there ain't nothing like that going on here. I just keep running.

Maybe she is lost or she will give up.

Moments later I see her out of the corner of my eye, I thought she was going to pass me up but she didn't. She was running beside me and started talking to me. By now we were on the 8 mile. A runner knows the mile marks that they struggle the most and they occupy themselves to move past that point. The 3rd to 4th mile is one of those points for me, also the 8th to 9th mile is another weak spot for me. I guess she was right on time to push me through the 8th mile. So I asked her if we could move up the pace a little, and she said sure, let's go.

Sometimes I say stuff without thinking, and regret what I said moments later. This was one of those times. All I can say is that mile a few by, she was just like Myra, she had that inner drive and I was thinking wow, I really need to ask that question tonight.

She stuck with me all the way to the finish line. When we got there, Myra and Larry were talking and laughing. Moments later Morgan showed up and she was laughing, too.

I felt like the elephant in the room, something going down and I'm not in the loop.

They set me up, and I guess she knew their plan. I laughed for a bit but then I had to stop. So I asked her what her name was and she said, "Zelia."

I said, "I would introduce myself but you probably know my name."

She said, "Ya, I do. I hope that's ok."

While we were walking back to the car I asked Myra if I could speak to her for a second.

She said, "Yeah what's up?"

I said, "How do you do it?"

She said, "Do what?"

I said, "What do you say to yourself that inspires you to blow past us so fast?"

She smiled and said, That's easy, Will. This running that we do every day, the training, the food choices we make to reach our goals. The key is you have to love the grind. That's why I can pass you up everyday of the week. I love the grind so much."

She went on to say that Jim Taylor Ph.D wrote an article In Psychology Today. "He talks about what separates athletes that achieve great things and those that don't.

"He said, 'In training and competitions, you arrive at a point at which it is no longer fun. I call this the Grind, which starts when it gets tiring, painful, and tedious. The Grind is also the point at which it really counts. The Grind is what separates successful athletes from those who don't achieve their goals. Many athletes when they reach this point either ease up or give up because it's just too darned hard. But truly motivated athletes reach the Grind and keep on going.'"

Myra looked at me and said, "To get to the next level you need someone to motivate you and run with you and you need to learn to love that grind. That's why Zelia is here. She will help you get there."

I got in my car and headed back home. I was thinking about what Myra had said, all the way home. I could clearly see the challenge I was facing to get to the next level. I had to love the grind. I have to be honest here and so do you. How much in love with the grind are you? I love the grind but maybe I'm not in with it. There is a difference you know.

Being with someone just because you love them gets old after a while. Being with someone because you're in love with them never gets old. This is exactly what Myra is talking about; she is in love with the grind, and I have to get to that same place. This will definitely be a challenge for me and it may be a challenge for you, too.

This is what I have been saying all along, Running for me is not about completing a half-marathon. Running is about the change, the challenges that need to take place in my life to cross the finish line.

They are right. I do need help to get to the next level. I have been doing this alone for way too long, I do need Zelia's help, I hope that she can get me there.

There are many different ways that friends, coaches, loved ones, colleges, push you to the next level.

So where are you on your journey? Is it the grind that keeps you from reaching your goal or are you at a point you need help? Are you like me: You love the grind but you're not in love with the grind?

In my effort to fall in love with the grind I wrote a short song that I sing as I run. I know that you can do a better job so write down your song below and let's move on to the next level.

The Grind Song

When you get to the point where it's no longer fun, and your love for the grind is done, done, done.

When Mr. Given up gets to know your first name, 'cuz this training challenge is driving you insane.

Remember the love for the grind is what separates us all, embrace the pain, embrace the wall.

Stay in this zone and soon you will see that the love for the grind will take you wherever you want to be.

Chapter 2

Well, it's Saturday and someone is knocking at my door. I opened the door to find the entire crew drinking coffee and pushing their way in the door. They said hurry up and get dressed 'cuz we are taking a road trip today. Ok, I grabbed a few things and out the door we went. We piled in the car and started down the road. Zelia told me we were headed to Phoenixville for the weekend. They were having two ten-mile runs, one on Saturday and the other on Sunday.

Myra, in her high-end outfit, spoke up and said "Will, here is your chance to win this weekend. None of us have run here before but you ran here last year. You know the course well." I heard her talking but it was hard to focus on what she was saying because I noticed that Larry was wearing a studded running outfit. Oh my gosh, he is wearing a designer running outfit. I didn't respond to Myra right away. I needed a moment to process Larry's outfit. Courtney started laughing because she saw my face.

Morgan wanted no part of this, but Zelia whispered something in my ear and I just started laughing. I had to bite my lip, and I turned to Myra quickly and said something like, "Wow, ya, I was here last year."

We got to the motel and Larry and I went to our room to drop off our luggage. I looked at Larry on the way up the elevator. I mean all the way up to the 5th floor. Larry asked me where we were going to eat. I said, "Stop, Larry. Where did you get that outfit?"

Larry said, "It's part of the new collection of designer running ware. I chose the studded running outfit for the trip. Tomorrow on our run I'm wearing the newest design. It's shiny purple and silver with a gray belt. The shirt is a little high and so are the shorts. The running shoes are shiny silver with purple laces." While Larry was talking to me I was in shock. I have to be honest here, I really didn't see that coming. Larry and I have talked about everything under the sun through the years since we were in high school and in just a few sentences I was looking at him saying to myself, who are you?

I just looked at Larry and said, "Ok, let's put the stuff in the room and go." Larry made eye contact with me and said, "Myra has been the best thing for me. I can do anything now and not worry about what people think and that's really what it's about."

He got serious for a minute and said that his greatest challenge through the years was worrying about what people think. I just sat down on the bed for a minute and listened. I was hearing this for the first time. It was really heavy to think that he felt he could never share anything like this with me before. I literally cried for a moment, because Larry and I have been friends for so long.

Wherever your journey leads you, there may be times that you need to hear the challenges of others. Don't be shocked, it may be someone close to you that needs to share something. Maybe something is challenging you and you may need to share that with someone. This is part of the process to get across the finish line. So take the time and listen, take the chance and share it with someone you trust.

We got down stairs and the girls were waiting to eat, it wasn't long after that and Larry and I were back in the room trying to sleep. When Larry sleeps he does this Alligator roll all night long. It drives me crazy. I can't sleep in the same bed because he takes all the covers.

I rolled over and listened to some music for a while; that helps sometimes. I started to think about Larry and then the next thing I knew the alarm was going off. I turned it off and jumped out of bed. I said to Larry get up, as I walked over to his pile of blankets and sheets. I looked but he wasn't there. I looked in the bathroom and no Larry. I got dressed and opened the door, as I headed toward the elevator I could see Larry and

Myra stretching and talking about the run. Myra is coaching Larry. I could hear her giving him some running advice. Ok, his outfit was kind of loud, and the shirt and shorts were too short. I was thinking of Richard Simmons at this point. I remember when ties were skinny then they went back to being fat, now they're back to being skinny again.

Fashion runs in cycles where they come and go. Maybe I'm just not with it. Maybe I need to update my running outfit.

Zelia grabbed me by the hand and said, "Let's go." She took me to the hotel exercise room and we started stretching. We were talking about some running strategies. She said, "I will set the pace for you. We are not going to start off fast. We are going to manage our energy. We are going to break the race up into segments. The first 3 miles are going to be a little slow, the next 4 miles are going to be a little faster, and the final 3 miles are going to be really fast. She said, "We will stop at the stations to refuel along the way, but stay by my side."

Zelia had me on Carbon 60 for the past few weeks along with Cordyceps. She doubled my vitamin C intake along with a dash of Turmeric sprinkled gracefully on my food. Oh, did I forget the pepper? Ok, a lot of pepper, too. She also designed my meals, and what I would be drinking on a daily basis. I have noticed a difference in my energy level. Zelia said, "It's time to grab some food before the run. We still have a few hours before the race. We need to load up on some carbs and relax for a moment."

We pushed the elevator button and as the door opened Zelia ran into some friends that she used to run with in South America. They were speaking Spanish. They were talking about the race. They had breakfast with us, and they ate a lot of food. They were very funny people.

We headed down to the starting line and it seemed like there were so many people.

Zelia leaned over to me and said, "Follow me." We pushed through the crowd and made it towards the front. I looked around to see if I could see anyone I knew but there were too many people. Zelia leaned over to me and said that Myra and Larry will break the race down into 3 miles segments and the last mile will be a sprint. "Remember the mile sprints we did? Well, that's why, because it's here that you're going to beat them. You will be ahead a little on your second segment, it will be 4 miles and you have to keep up with me. We need that lead because Myra's last mile is too fast and we won't be able to beat her."

Suddenly someone touched my left shoulder, I turned around and it was Morgan. She said, "I will help you with your pace, too, but I won't be able to keep that pace past the 7 mile." I have to admit that I was feeling a lot of pressure to perform at my best in this race. I was starting to feel a little anxiety.

I don't know how professional athletes do it, the pressure, anxiety that must build up before a game. Really the fans come to see you perform. If you make a home run, they like you. If you miss the ball, they boo you.

Brian Urlacher, a "Former Chicago Bears linebacker would eat two chocolate chip cookies before each game, and he'd eat them while listening to country music." I'm not sure how that takes off the pressure but it must work for him 'cuz he is making the big bucks.

I just click on the Doobie Brothers, I try to keep it simple, although the cookies and country music sounds pretty basic. Find something that works for you and just do it.

This is something that you don't want to over think. It's just a distraction, like the dentist telling you a joke just before he yanks out your tooth.

It was time for the race. The announcer came on and introduced a few people, then he started the countdown. Zelia on my right and Morgan on my left, I closed my eyes for a moment and visualized the race. I could see the course in my head, every street, every bridge, every hill. Myra was right. I do have an advantage.

The buzzer went off and we took off running. It was tight between runners for the first hundred feet, then we each had a little room to breathe. We were heading down a hill and soon we would be taking a left up a long hill. I paced alongside Zelia and when we took that left I was ready for the hill. I shortened my steps and up we went to the top.

Zelia looked surprised, but she didn't say a word. Morgan looked a little wiped but that was a long hill. We were on our third mile and it was time to shift gears. I felt Zelia picking up the pace. The road leveled off for a bit but I knew after the turn ahead we would be going down hill for at least a mile. I wanted to use this time to conserve my energy so I took some long strides. I kept taking deep breaths, and I opened a pack of gels. I like the brand GU, It seems to give me the fuel I need quickly. Gels are simple sugars which your body prefers during exercise. I didn't really need it at this point but I wanted to be prepared for Zelia's pace. We headed for the bridge, and it got real tight there. All the runners merge together to cross the bridge because the bridge is not very wide. The last time I ran across the bridge I was so close to the wall my earphones caught on a nail and were ripped from my head, I didn't even look back, I just kept running.

I leaned over to Zelia and said, "The bridge is ahead and we will have to merge together, it's tight."

She said, “Follow me.” We moved to the middle of the crowd and easily pushed through crossing the bridge. We took a right after crossing the bridge and headed downtown. I looked at my app, we had just cleared 7 miles. I turned to see where Morgan was and she was still there. I yelled over to her, “Will you make it?” She grabbed her left wrist and put her hand around it. Then she touched her head. She was saying, “I think so but it will be tough.”

We were headed for the railroad tracks and I knew what was coming next. We would pass the brewery head up a long hill then take a left up another hill to the park. It’s that second hill that kills you. The last time I ran here I gave 100 percent on that first hill and I had nothing left for the second hill to the park. Zelia tapped me and pointed to Myra and Larry. They were making their way through the crowd but we were still ahead. We just passed the brewery and I knew we only had a mile and a half left. Zelia looked at me and shouted, “Let’s go.”

The brewery hill is almost a mile. The second hill is about a half of a mile before you get to the park. I leaned over to her and I said that we need to save a little energy for the second hill. I didn’t think she heard me but a moment later she said ok. The last thing I wanted was to get passed up by Larry in his designer running outfit so I turned around and got their attention and waved at them with a big smile. Larry and Myra started running so fast by the time they got to the top of the hill they were beside us and out of breath. Zelia laughed ‘cuz she knew that I got the designer couple to burn up all their energy and here comes the second hill. I knew Myra was capable of passing us up so I put on a song that takes me to another place, I put on Elton John, “The Rocket Man”. I started sprinting uphill faster than I had ever run. My heart was beating so loud that it drowned out every noise around me. I came up over the hill and I could see the park. I knew that the finish line was right there. I had 40 feet to go. I leaned forward and gave what I had left. After crossing the finish line, I turned around and stared at the people coming across the finish line. I could see Zelia and behind her I could see Myra then Larry. The designer couple was exhausted and so was Zelia. We were cheering Morgan on as she fell across the finish. She got up and started laughing. She said the line was too high.

Larry said, “Come on, girl, are you ok?”

She said, “Let’s get some food to eat.” We headed toward the concession stand, laughing about the day. Zelia looked at me and smiled. She said, “Where did you get that burst of energy from, Will?”

I said, “It just happened.”

Just when you think you will never break through, it happens. Look at Reggie

Jackson, struck out 2600 times in his career, the most in the history of baseball. All everyone remembers is the home runs. This was a home run for me and a start to a new beginning.

The next week we met at Larry's dealership. The girls were in the bathroom changing. Larry was looking for the keys of a new car he got this past week. He was going to take me for a ride. I was looking at the sticker price of a car in the showroom when Myra said, "Will, you took me by surprise last weekend. I just wanted to tell you. I don't know how you did it but great job." I was going to say something to her but Larry grabbed me by the arm and pushed me in a car. He said, "You can tell her later." Down the road we went for another test drive.

I looked at Larry and said, "All the hours I have put in running and working out has not guaranteed that I would beat Myra. Each workout has brought me closer to winning, but last week I finally made it."

Chapter 3

We just landed in Costa Rica and a taxi picked us up, took us to Don Francisco's.

It's a great place to stay for a few days. I love it because it is so comfortable. It is the perfect getaway spot. It's located in Escazu, and it is a laid back community with a lot of hills. This is the perfect place for some practice runs. We got up in the morning and made some coffee and food. I love my sweet potatoes. If you cook them in the oven, and then stick them in the fridge overnight they become resistant starch, and they don't get absorbed until they get to the large colon. Ok, what's that all that about? Well, layman's terms, it keeps you skinny. You don't gain much weight from eating them. I don't want to bore you but everyone here has their own meal plan. When we are all in the same kitchen it can be a little difficult making breakfast. We all have our opinions about food and what works best for us and that's cool. I have mine and I try to stick to it when I can.

This is my 4th year here. I first came to Costa Rica to get some dental work done, but I keep coming back in the summer because it was so enjoyable. It's the place that I feel at home the most. I have run these mountains for several years. We are racing in Baltimore in a few weeks and this is the place to get you ready for those Baltimore hills.

Yes, Baltimore has a lot of hills, especially when you go around the lake and head back to the finish line. You hit hill after hill. If you're not ready for that it will pull your bones down to the pavement.

Well, the girls are completing their morning brunch. Larry is eating brunch, too. We are ready to head out for our first practice run. Larry and I led the girls down the road toward route 130 and we headed towards highway 27. It's down hill some, lots of cars to watch out for and the ditches are unforgivable. If you fall in the ditch we will pick you up on the way back.

After we cross 27 the hills get steep. They make you feel like you just ran across Texas.

I ask Zelia to step up beside me and take the lead for a moment. Two weeks of this and your legs feel like timbers. Zelia was breathing heavily, so were the rest of the crew, I knew that we would have to stop soon. We took a break at the top of a hill and the view was spectacular. We headed home and Morgan took the lead. She is into her running equipment, she is always changing out her shoes.

As a general rule Runner's World Magazine says you should "change your running shoes between 300 to 500 miles." You may not be aware how far you travel each day in your shoes, but the life of a shoe only seems long because you keep wearing them.

Stop it, look at the bottom of them, if there is no tread on them throw them away.

If you don't change them out you will increase stress and impact on your legs and joints. So if you're doing a lot of running, think about updating your equipment.

Myra stepped up with Morgan and the pace got real. I was ready for it, as we raced all the way back home. Larry stepped out on the street to pass Zelia, I guess he didn't see the motorcycle 'cuz he blew his horn and Larry jumped back across the ditch. We laughed and kept running. I grabbed hold of Courtney's arm as she was drifting toward the ditch. Heading up the hill we were all at a full sprint. It's funny because most of the sidewalks don't go straight. They go around a tree, or something crazy, so you have to pay attention. Myra was in the lead, but Larry was about to pass her. He didn't follow the sidewalk, he jumped out on the street and kept on going. We were all watching because this was about to get very interesting.

How would Myra handle it if Larry passed her during a full sprint up hill? In front of everyone. Love or no love, Larry was bringing it home. We drifted in behind Larry like we were trying to get into the store before it closed. Everyone one was sweating, when we got home my clothes were ringing wet. Tomorrow is going to be an interesting day. We all have something to prove and that's what makes up a team. We challenge each other daily. I like what William Frederick Halsey, Jr. said, "There are no great people in this world, only great challenges which ordinary people rise to meet."

The second day is here. After yesterday I can feel the competition, not really but it's how everyone is looking at each other. It's that serious look. Sometimes I have to walk away and laugh. I ate light and drank plenty of fluids. I have a small pouch I strap on my side.

I put some water in a plastic bag and stuck it in the pouch. In a pinch is just enough to get me home. We were all in front of the house ready to start. Larry counted down from 10 and when he hit 4 everyone took off. Larry was still going to wait till he hit 1 because that's how he is with everything.

I yelled from a distance, "Larry, come on everyone is gone." Larry took off, passed me by and yelled, "Come on, Will." I took off running on the streets of Escazu. Nothing is more exciting than 6 people racing on the streets passing cars, crossing streets, jumping over the ditches, coasting through the lights and talking to each other along the way. Before we got to highway 27 there was a line of people waiting at the bakery, the line went out into the street. I leaned forward and yelled out every Spanish word I knew, to excuse me, Perdon, con permiso, lo siento, fue sin querer. I felt like Moses parting the Red Sea.

A hole the size your refrigerator opened up and we all ran through. We had to make our way through the cars coming off the ramp. Some were stopped but others kept going without stopping. Myra, Larry, Morgan made it through, Courtney, Zelia and I had to wait. Finally we made it through, we were trying to catch up to the others running uphill.

A car pulled out of the shopping center and slowed Myra, Larry and Morgan down for a second. They started to go behind the car and another car pulled into the parking lot and cut them off. It was a gift from above because we were right behind them. There was a lot of high grass on each side of the sidewalk, it was like running through a cornfield at night. After we all made it through the grass the sidewalk opened up and we were all trying to pass each other. Yesterday we were at this point and needed to take a break, today no break in sight, just a lot of pain. Some cars were coming so everyone jumped back on the sidewalk. There was a bus picking up people ahead, it looked like you could get caught up for a second if you ran into the crowd. I headed back on the street, I was going around the bus even if I had to squeeze between the bus and the traffic. This was my chance to pull ahead. Zelia followed me, around the bus we went, at some point it was tight, we slowed down a bit but made it through. Zelia and I were finally ahead, and I didn't feel like I needed to check on the rest of the crew.

We made it to the turn around point, it was 5 miles. We wasted no time heading back.

Zelia said, "We can beat them, Will, let's kick it up a little." Zelia had these long legs, her stride was huge. I just had to figure out how I could keep up with her. My legs felt strong, I pulled out that bag of water, I drank some and gave the rest to Zelia. The sweat was rolling off me, I could feel my body heating up. Zelia's shirt was drenched. I took off my shirt and threw it on the sidewalk. I hoped my body would start to cool down. Myra came up beside wearing a designer outfit and tossed her shirt, too. Well, if that didn't start a trend because Zelia peeled hers off, too. It's pretty common with us; we just throw it aside if it's not working.

We topped the hill and headed down the other side. The sidewalks were wide so we ran together for a bit but heading up the hill again I jumped out on the street because there were a lot of mom and pop shops close to the sidewalks and I didn't want to run into anyone. It was down the hill, across the bridge, up the hill past McDonalds, up the hill again, take a left and then a right, head down that last stretch to the house and we would be home. When we crossed the bridge Larry and Courtney passed us rather fast.

I yelled out, "What's the hurry, guys?"

I knew this was it, there was a stoplight up ahead with a road to the left. Cars were lined up there and I could only see one option. Cross the street and keep going up the hill. I yelled, "Myra, follow me." Cars were traveling up and down the street fast. Did I say that there were motorcycles also, they are hard to see? As all three of us crossed the street we almost got clipped by a few bikes, but we were fast and headed up the hill past McDonalds. We had one more hill left. I was already thinking we needed to slow down for a few seconds, get some air and head to the finish line. Taking the right went fast but crossing the street to take the left was scary. We all crossed together and headed towards the finish line.

Sometimes I wish that I was the only one that could see the finish line, because here is where things get crazy. Several people running in the same direction looking at several people running in the same direction. I am sure that you can figure out what happens next, but for those who can't.... It's an all out screamer all the way to the finish line.

When we got back, we ate a lot of food, we got into the car and drove around sightseeing. We went to Puntarenes, Jaco beach and a few shops along the way.

We ran through the mountains together for the next two weeks, and traveled around the country. We were leaving in the morning, and we were ready for Baltimore.

I believe in dreaming about doing great things, setting goals that seem difficult to achieve, and changing my life up when things get too comfortable. This is exciting and this is what great people do.

I read an article in Quora by Vinoth Xavier. He was talking about the Sistine Chapel. He said that, " Michelangelo began work on the ceiling in July 1508. The completed frescoes were unveiled in October 1512. The chapel's paintings cover 12,000 sq ft (1,110 sq m), about one-sixth the size of a football pitch.

Contrary to Myth, Michelangelo did not paint on his back, but on a platform of his own devising that extended over half the area of the chapel and allowed him to stand upright.

It was moved midway through the project.

At no point could Michelangelo look at the work in progress from below, but he was still able to paint images on a vast scale from a distance of a few inches.

How crazy is that? It means that he was painting the ceiling above and could not view it from below because of the scaffolding. Half way through they took down the scaffolding and he could finally see his work. He was able to visualize his work from the beginning to the end without seeing his completed work until he was half way through. Can you close your eyes and visualize each workout you complete, taking you to that final place of success?

Can you see each workout you struggle through as a great work of art?

I wonder if he ordered some food and a glass of wine and just stared at his work for a bit.

I wonder if he said to himself that's not exactly what I was trying to paint. Or if he stood in amazement at his work, every swipe of the brush, every unique color he created captured the story he was trying to tell.

We may never know what he thought, but we do know that if we don't dream about amazing things and write amazing stories about our lives and try to live them we will have nothing to look at all.

The second point I want to share is that Michelangelo was not just painting for a local pope, he was painting for Pope Julius II. This pope regained the lost Papal lands, which made him one of the most powerful men in the world. He rode into battle to join the struggle for the Papal lands. He was nicknamed the "Warrior Pope, the terrible pope due to his famous bad temper."

And yet Michelangelo had confidence in himself and his ability to create a great work without fear. If anyone should be wearing a shirt that says NO FEAR, it should have been him.

This is important because we need to be confident in ourselves in order to move forward. We can't spend a lot of time second guessing ourselves. We don't have a lot of time here on earth. We must paint our lives quickly with confidence and then live them out with splendor. Don't let fear hold you back from life.

Chapter 4

"Breaking through the fog" was the heading of an article written about Florence Chadwick by the Women's Museum of California. The article said, "In 1952 Florence attempted to swim from California mainland to Catalina Island. After 15 hours an immense fog prevented her from seeing the finish line and she called it quits."

After being pulled into the boat she discovered if she had just continued on for another mile she would have reached Catalina Island.

The takeaway from this story for me is, don't focus on the fog, keep your eyes on the finish line. I mean really how many of us have thrown in the towel on our dreams just before it was about to happen.

What is the fog? It's all those things that keep you from seeing the finish line.

For me it's the chatter that goes on in my head like self doubt, confidence, fear, rethinking my ability to dream so big that it may not happen.

The fog usually appears when I am standing at the starting line surrounded by thousands of people. I'm thinking out of all these people what are the odds that I will place decently. That's where reality reaches out and confronts you. It looks you in the eyes and keeps on staring at you until you look away. Don't look away, focus on the finish line.

Today we are in Baltimore, already unpacked, fed and sound asleep, everyone except Larry and I. I was up thinking about the race in the morning, I was trying to visualize the race. I had learned so much this year about overcoming challenges. My goal was to run 13.1 miles in an hour and forty five minutes. If I couldn't achieve that in Baltimore, there was one more race left, that was Norfolk, Va.

It seemed like only a few minutes passed, and then Larry was yelling at me to get up.

He usually jumps on me first, then beats me with a pillow, then he yells at me to get up.

I wish he would yell first, that way I could yell back at him before he jumps on me.

I jumped out of bed. I heard someone knocking on the door. I just stood there for a moment. I needed a second to wake up. I opened the door thinking the girls would be standing there with coffee for us, and it was Ruffin. The high school gym teacher. I was happy to see him.

Everyone went downstairs for breakfast. We ran into some more of Zelia's friends, one was called Marshmallow and the other was called Garbanzos. I'm not asking how they got their names, because they looked like they were life marathoners. Frankly I do want to know why two marathoners are named after food products but sometimes the juice ain't worth the squeeze. Besides, how many friends does she have anyways? After we ate we headed to the starting line. It was early, we had about 2 hours before the race.

Marshmallow came over to help us stretch. Then Garbanzos warmed us up with a few short sprints. Did you ever feel like there are a lot of people helping you to get to the finish line?

But really the only person that can get you there is you. I hope you hear me. After warming up we sat for a bit and listened to Marshmallow talk about his last race. We were all pumped up. Myra and Larry got up and danced a bit for us. Courtney laughed and jumped in with Morgan. Before we knew it 20 people were dancing to the tune of Play that Funky Music White Boy.

Lucky for the race announcer the song stopped when Myra dropped her phone.

We were so loud I think he was looking for an in to start the race. We walked over to line up, it's a lot of people in one spot, with running clothes on, and some people go all out and dress up as some character. Marshmallow and Garbanzos got in front of us. We were all behind them except for

Ruffin. With the last minute counting down, I was looking to the right at all the people standing in line at the port-a-potties. I was wondering if they were going to make it. We were starting in under a minute. Zelia said at the last moment, follow us and don't get lost.

The bell went off, the first wave of runners took off; we were in the second wave waiting.

The second wave took off running. It seemed like we were running slow at first but Marshmallow, Garbanzos broke to the side and headed up Light St. Zelia reached back and grabbed me by the hand. I was fighting my way out of the crowd. We made it just in time to turn right on Baltimore street. Our next turn would be at the park over a mile away. I was keeping up with Zelia's crew. it didn't surprise me at all. All those hills I ran in Costa Rica my legs felt like huge timbers. They felt kind of bulky, I noticed my compact pants were tighter than before I came to Costa Rica. Did I tell you that I bought a designer running outfit off of Myra?

Well, you know what they say, if you hang around the barbershop long enough you're bound to get a haircut. That saying is a little overused but there may still be some life left in it. Anyways, you get my point. I told her if she could design an outfit like Michael Johnson's I would wear it in Baltimore. I was at the Olympics in '96, I watched Johnson beat Fredericks in the 200 meter. He was wearing Nike gold shoes with a blue and white outfit. Johnson had become the first man in history to complete the 200 meters in under 20 seconds. I watched him make history; I watched him cross the finish line.

I could see the park ahead. Zelia was moving over to the left with her boys, and I followed. I knew coming out of the park was the third mile and I had to be prepared to mentally hold on till I got to the fourth mile. The third to fourth mile has always been tough for me. It is usually all in my head, but I need to move beyond that during this race or I will fall behind.

If you stop to think about your challenges, don't brush them off, use them, get to know them, admit that they are there and overcome them. Ruffin always says you have to be honest with yourself.

Taking a right and two lefts around the park doesn't seem hard on paper but running with a group of people shifting from one side of the road to the other is difficult. I get distracted at times because people are talking to each other, bystanders are holding up signs shouting, and you bump into someone that is blind running beside you with his guide team.

Coming out of the park on that last turn I could see Larry and Myra. Myra was pointing at my outfit and laughing. Larry just looked the other way. I know he was laughing too.

Everyone shifted my way. I was being pinched up against a retainer wall. it was about three feet high. Zelia looked back at me and shook her head. Ok, maybe I should have been paying attention instead of looking at Larry but here I was stuck behind Mr. Slow.

I looked at the wall without even thinking. I pushed up as hard as I could with my left leg and I lifted my right leg. Before you knew it I ran down the wall to an opening past Zelia and her friends. I jumped down in an opening and kept on running. I was into the fourth mile and that little move lifted my soul. I was in the lead and I was not about to look back. I took a left on Madison street and kept on running.

When I got to Washington I took a right and headed for the park. it's uphill for a bit, then you circle the lake. I was ready for the hills. I ran a ton of hills in Costa Rica, and they would not slow me down. I heard Ruffin calling my name. I looked to the right and he was just coming out of the port-a- potties. We ran together to the lake. Running around the lake seems like it takes forever but it's a good place to look for people that are on your team. I spotted Zelia and Marshmallow but I didn't see anyone else. It was too crowded. I could feel my body overheating. I had been pushing my body so hard. I stopped for a drink at the water station and ripped open a pack of GU Energy Gel. I needed some carbs to keep my body moving.

I was getting ready to hit the eighth mile and I was running strong. If you run you know what the eighth mile feels like, you're not exhausted but you're really not fresh either.

When I get this far I need to stay focused on what I need to be doing at this point in the run. Every minute counts and I can't afford to lose one minute. I was looking for some help when half way through the eighth mile Zelia caught up with me. She said slow down a little, your pace is too fast. Marshmallow and Garbanzos moved up beside me, too. Garbanzos said follow my lead, so I moved in behind him only because he has more letters in his name than mine. Zelia said, "I was shocked that you took the wall. It was the only move you had and you took it."

I said, "I didn't even think about it. I just knew that I needed to get to the finish line fast and it was my only door. Sometimes you know what you can do, just do it."

I was getting thirsty; my body needed water. I knew there was a water station at 33rd Street that would be the ninth mile. My mind was trying to tell me to stop.

Just as I was drifting with that idea, the rest of the crew showed up. Courtney had some water. I took a sip. Morgan laughed, “Wow, you are really working up a sweat, Will.” I was happy to see them again, running together brings so much strength.

Chapter 5

Always trust your gut. It knows what your head hasn't figured out yet. That's not my quote, it came from Quora.com but I wish I had written that line because it holds a lot of truth. Reaching the water station at the ninth mile, I picked up some gels in different forms and a banana. I knew what was ahead, Maryland Ave. Last time I was running on that street I felt like the kids in the back seat of the car. I kept asking myself, are we there yet, are we there yet. It felt like it took forever to get to the end of it.

When I left the ninth mile water station, I had been thinking about picking up my pace till I got to the 10 mile and then sprinting to the finish line. I had been running for the past two years all year around. I ran in the rain, in the snow, and in the cold weather. Did you ever have a time during one of your difficult workouts you said to yourself, why are you doing this, what is this about. Just go home and sit on the couch and watch T.V.

There was one time I went for a run, it looked like it was going to rain so I wore a raincoat. It was in the fall and the wind was picking up. I was 7 miles in my run and it started to pour down. I turned around and was trying to get home as soon as possible, but the wind and rain pounded down on me. By the time I got home I was physically and mentally exhausted. So for me finishing this race strong was not just something I wanted, it was something I owed to myself. It for all those sidewalks covered in snow, it was for the several layers of clothes I loaded up on during my winter runs, it was for all those times I had to run in the dark, it was for all those car that almost ran over me and there were many that came close.

I started to pick up the pace. I actually passed up Marshmallow, Zelia and the rest. I saw the tenth mile marker and I looked over to the left and Myra was right behind me. Did you ever feel like you were not the only one making plans? She was going to sprint to the finish line, too. The only difference is she could do it. I saw her do it many times before. I waited till I passed the ten mile mark and then I kicked it in high gear.

I was trying to stay on the right side of the road so I wouldn't bump into anyone. Then all of a sudden someone in front of me fell. It was a girl in her twenties. I stopped to see if she was ok and she said yes. I picked up the pace while looking for Myra. I lost her and I didn't know where she went.

Garbanzos tapped me on the shoulder and said, "Let go. If you want to sprint all out to the finish line, let's do it together." When we hit the tenth mile there was a crowd ahead.

We started to slow down. People on the sidelines were giving free food and drinks and it really drew a crowd. I looked to the left and there was a small opening. Garbanzos yelled over here and just like that I was undecided which way to go. My gut feeling said go with him, so I turned and followed him.

We ran up over the sidewalk, jumped over a border fence and crossed between a row of Forsythias and back on the road. Who do you think we ran into doing the same thing, Myra. We were coming up to the water station on the eleventh mile. I really wasn't thirsty but Garbanzos said to stop and get some Gatorade to drink. I grabbed a glass and kept on running. I knew that we had a little over two miles left to go to the finish line.

I had to outperform Myra, not only physically but mentally, too.

This is what I have been saying all along. Running for me is not about completing a half-marathon, running is about the change, the challenges that need to take place in my life to cross the finish line. In life your challenge may not be trying to beat Myra, although it would be a worthy goal, I know. It may be passing a class, losing weight, starting a business, or just learning to get along with a coworker. Whatever you challenge here me out. There is a way to win, you just have to find it.

I had to beat her at her own game and it wasn't going to be pretty. That's why I have been running the mountains for the past few months. Just like Myra was planning things all along, so was I. I took off running as fast as I could. After a while I could feel pain in my legs. Next my lungs started to burn, and then I could feel my body start to heat up. I wasn't shocked, all those mountain runs had introduced me into this process over and over again. I could stop the lungs from burning by taking longer breaths, instead of gulping in a lot of air. The rest was going to have to wait till the finish line.

I was on my last mile and I was cruising, I had no desire to look back. I could see the boats and I could hear the people cheering, I knew that it was just around the bend.

Garbanzos ran up beside me and I looked over at him, just for a moment I knew what he was going to say, Myra is right behind you. I was out of options, my brain was not even thinking anymore. In fact my body was in the process of shutting down. Do you know when your phone starts to die and you look at it while the screen goes black and you say crap. I was at that spot, till Garbanzos yelled at me, he said, "Wake up and start taking longer strides. You're bigger than her and you cover more ground."

I started breathing deep breaths, and taking long strides all the way across the finish line. I ran for another 30 feet and then fell on the grass and looked at the sky for a few minutes. It was so peaceful, until Myra jumped on me screaming.

She said she was just happy for me, but we all know that she was freaking mad. Soon Larry showed up and pulled her off of me. The rest came over and sat down beside me and we laughed and looked at the sky together. I had never pushed my body so hard. I just wanted to stay there for a while and rest. Have you ever been there where you just can't move? You know that you need to get up but you just don't care. I was there just looking up at the clouds enjoying the chatter I was hearing around me.

Chapter 6

In case you don't know what the weather is like in November, I will just say it's cold. Lots of people like the different seasons but I'm not one of those people. The hotter the weather the more I feel at home. Besides who wants to rake leaves, anyways. So what do you wear to run in the winter time? Everything you can put on in 15 minutes. Not a big fan of this activity. The good news is in the morning, the running crew is going to Virginia to do the Harbor Run. It is one of my favorites, because while everyone up north is raking leaves and wearing coats, those in the south are still hanging on to the warm weather. I have everything packed, all I have to do is pretend that I am sleeping for eight hours, get up and meet everyone at Larry's dealership.

I had a glass of wine and some chicken, and I'm ready for bed. I set my alarm because I hate to be late and it was lights out. I was enjoying my last two victories. I didn't lay in bed gloating about them but it taught me if you keep trying you will succeed.

Joyce Myers says, "You don't know the sweet till you taste the sour." Man if that doesn't hit home. You can't fully appreciate the victory of a win until you have experienced failure. So when you fail, embrace it, don't give up. It is part of the process that will make you enjoy your victory. Get up and keep on going.

Hearing the alarm clock go off was music to my ears. I just put on some coffee and I heard someone knocking on the door. I swung open the door way too quickly 'cuz someone was selling cookies. I thought, wow this is going to take a few minutes. Just as they were winding up for this big sales pitch, I said, "I'm in a hurry, save the pitch just give me a few boxes." When I took a second glance I noticed that the young man was dressed up in running clothes. I said, "Where are you going in those clothes?"

He said, "My name is Antxon and I'm leaving shortly to go to Virginia."

I said, Really, what's there?"

He said, "I'm running in the marathon in Norfolk."

I said, Really, that's pretty amazing, I will be there too. I hope that I see you there." I noticed that everyone was laughing and so I started laughing too. Then I stopped and said, "Ok what's so funny?"

Antxon said, "I will be riding with you." I paused for a moment, so the caffeine could kick in, 'cuz I didn't get the memo. Suddenly the phone rang and it was Zelia. She hesitated for a moment and cleared her throat. I don't know why it took so long but she finally said that her son would be riding with me. I said, "Is his name Antxon?"

She said, "Yes, he should be at your door soon but don't buy the cookies."

Antxon stepped inside while I was getting ready to go. We threw everything in the truck and we headed for the dealership. Antxon and I just rattled about some small talk and when we got to the dealership he stepped out of the truck and hugged his mom. It felt good to add one more person to the running family.

Larry fired up his motor home, everyone jumped in and we all picked on Antxon for a few miles. Antxon was tall and he ran track in high school and college. He took a semester off from school and came to live with his mom for a year. He was going to school on an athletic scholarship.

The trip went so fast, and before you knew it we were there. Antxon followed Larry and I to the room. We ordered another bed, threw our stuff down and went to the lobby to meet the girls. Zelia shouted who wants to eat crabs, I know a hole in the wall where the food rocks. We all piled in and took off for the joint. It was on a side street, surrounded by boats. We jumped out and headed in the joint and sat down. The waiter rolled out a sheet of paper and put it on the table. We ordered crabs, and ate crabs for an hour. She was right, this was a hole in the wall but the food was excellent.

I ordered some rice and beans to carb up for the race in the morning and so did Antxon.

We got back to the room and I got tucked in ASAP. I was going to try to fall asleep before Larry came to bed. I told Antxon you should go to bed ASAP, too. He looked at me and said why? I said, "Ok good night, and we can talk about it in the morning."

Sometimes I just don't have the energy to explain things anymore. I heard the alarm clock going off and I jumped out of bed. I took a long shower and put my gear on for the run. I went downstairs to grab some food and coffee. I just wanted to be alone for a minute and think about the run. I didn't know how the run was going to go today so I felt really nervous.

Zelia came down in her PJs to get some coffee and she said, "What's up, Will?"

"I'm just a little worried about today's run."

She said, "What else is going on, Will?"

I said, "Have you ever looked at your life carefully? Most people look at their life and say it really sucks, or they like their life. I have been looking at my life carefully. I have been looking at who I am, and I came to the conclusion that I love the way I am. I realized it when we were in Costa Rica, I wrote it in the sand when we were on the beach in Spanish, me amo como soy. The relationship that I have with myself is the most important relationship that I will ever have in my life and how often do we think about that."

A lot of people like me wake up and realize that they don't like who they are in life, and I get that, but they don't have to stay at that place. I mean I haven't always liked who I am. They have the power to change just like me. I have changed and that change has brought me to that place where I have peace with myself and who I am. I took a sip of my coffee and looked up at Zelia and I noticed tears running down her face. I grabbed her hand as we both sat there for a moment crying. The rest of the crew came down and sat beside us chatting away. I let go of Zelia's hand and we got up to get some more coffee. It's kind of weird to say but I felt cleansed while sharing my thoughts with Zelia.

I was ready now to focus on the race but I was not alone. Myra, Antxon, Larry, Zelia, Courtney, and Morgan were all focused on the race. We finished eating and headed up to our rooms for a minute. Larry and Antxon were chatting about cars as we got off the elevator. Myra and the girls were chatting about their new running shoes. Less than an hour later we were standing around at the starting line laughing about my running glasses.

I got them in Norfolk last year and they were free. They looked kind of funky but they are my favorite pair of sunglasses. They are big and blue and kind of bulky. I usually lose a pair each year but I have managed to keep these for some time, thank God.

We were lined up on Waterside drive, a lot of people gathered around the starting line, there were some announcements going on for a while. From a runners point of view, you are packed close together with other runners all waiting for the same thing, the announcements to end. How long can you stand next to someone dressed like Mickey Mouse, or Joan of Arc. Finally the announcements ended and the 5 minute clock to start the race began. We all looked at each other, and for a moment we laughed, I said, “I hope you all can keep up with me, ‘cuz I’m giving it 100% today.”

Myra laughed and said to me, “Is that all you’re giving? I will pass you up and win the race because I love the grind. I will be given more than 100 %.” Antxon and Zelia just laughed at them, because they were eating most of the cookies I bought from Antxon on the trip down to Norfolk. Zelia said, “By the time your sugar high wears off, we will be making our first turn on Saint Paul’s Boulevard.” Courtney and Morgan just got in line to run, shaking their heads.

One minute to go and I was checking everything. Antxon told me that my mom and I will follow you, you set the pace for the first four miles, I will pick up the next four miles and my mom will take the last four. After that we are all on our own. I said, "That sounds great, let's do it." Just then the bell went off and runners started to cross the starting line. It's not like we all start running at once. We were in the fourth wave this time and it took a few minutes to get going. Finally we started moving, but there was not much room to run.

After a few hundred feet we were able to spread out some and I took the lead. By the time we got to East Olney Road we were headed into the second mile. I looked back over my shoulder, Zelia and Antxon were right behind me. I looked around for the rest of the crew but I only saw Morgan. I didn't want to be over confident, I heard Myra loud and clear at the starting line, she loves the grind and that could be something to worry about close to the finish line but I have no idea what Antxon can do so I need to focus on him during the last few miles. If Antxon and his mom kick it in early I will have no choice but to kick it in myself. Either way, I am ready to go.

When I said I'm ready to go that reminded me about an article I read on the race to the South Pole between Ronald Amundsen and Robert Falcon Scott. After reading about each one's strategies you can clearly see why Amunden won: He was better prepared. "He was only focused on reaching the south pole and returning home safely", nothing else.

My takeaway from the story is that once you prepare for the race, just focus on crossing the finish line, nothing else. I had no idea what Antxon was capable of but I knew what I was capable of and I was going to focus on that only.

We passed Pembrook Ave, we were now passing the third mile. This mile is a straight shot all the way down to Shirley Ave. I know once I get there I will take a left and start my fourth mile. I could hear Antxon tell his mom that Larry was moving through the crowd with Myra. Just then Myra spotted me and gave a shout out, "Will, how is that grind doing?" I looked over and smiled then kicked it up a little. I heard Courtney and Morgan laughing, I turned to them and said, "Did you hear that? She is something else." We were all there running for the finish line and she was only worried about me.

Antoxon moved up beside me and said, "I got it for the next four miles." I stepped in behind him. Zelia moved over toward me and said, "You know that Myra is just messing with your head? She is just getting into position. She won't make her move till after the tenth mile." I said, "I know but this race is different from the others. She lost the last two races. Myra is going to change up her strategy to throw me off and I am ready for it."

I didn't tell anyone but I already had a plan. I had been working all summer on increasing my endurance and I was ready for the long sprint to the finish line.

Antxon had two more miles to lead us and then Zelia would take the lead. I knew I could trust her and her son but I knew that he was young and fast and held many records in high school and college. I was not sure when we got to the last part of the race if I could keep up.

We finally got to West 43rd street and Zelia took the lead. I leaned over to Antxon and said, "We need to go faster. This pace is too slow."

Antxon said to his mom, "Mom, can you take it up some?" Just then Courtney and Morgan passed us up. Courtney yelled, "Follow us, guys. Let's burn through this crowd." Courtney was a trainer, she knew how to push her clients when she needed results. I knew that she might not make it to the finish line but she would push us all the way past the tenth mile.

I just kept thinking of what the ending of the race might look like. Along the way a lot of things can happen. Courtney was blasting through the crowd. There was a bottleneck ahead and she jumped up on the curb onto a supermarket sidewalk. People walking in and out made it tough to avoid the people traffic. I am not sure if it was part of the course but we made it through the bottleneck. I wanted to look for Larry and Myra but I knew they were not too far behind. While we passed the University village students were cheering us on and they came right out on the street. We picked up some food and drinks from the students. It was crazy good. Before we knew it we were at Powhatan Avenue running like hell. I took a quick look at Zelia and she was sweating so much that her shirt was transparent. I told her that we needed to stop at the next water station. You need to ditch that shirt and drink as much water as you can.

It wasn't just Zelia, all of us were feeling it. Even her son was feeling it which made me feel secure at this point in the race. We stopped at the next water station and drank some Gatorade and took some GU gel packets. I tossed my shirt along with Zelia, and we all took off for the 8th mile.

Let's talk about your vision, your dreams, something you need to achieve in your bucket list, whatever category you place it in, how will it end?

I would say it depends. It depends on how much you want it. It depends on your preparation. When you worked out, did you give a 100 percent or 40 percent? It depends on if you have plan B to fall back on in case plan A doesn't work out. It depends on if you allow fear to keep you from achieving your dreams.

If you want to win you have to follow those who have won. Joan of Arc was bold and fearless. She refused to take no for an answer. Michelangelo believed in himself and in his ability to create a great work of art. He was able to visualize his work from the beginning to the end without seeing it from a distance. Cortez burned the boats when he landed to defeat the Inca empire. What a statement he made; he had no plans on failing. He knew how it would end, in victory or death.

After leaving the water station Zelia glanced at me for a moment and said, "You need to take off when we hit the ninth mile and don't look back. If you get a head start Myra will not be able to catch you. Antxon can help you make it to the end but you need to follow him, and listen to what he says." When we got to the ninth mile Antxon took the lead, we were headed toward Gate Avenue. There were a lot of people on the streets holding up signs. There were a lot of lefts and rights, a lot of people slowing down, people talking to each other and then there was us just weaving around the obstacles. We were bouncing from side to side going through the streets.

I wanted to look around but I remembered what Zelia said, "Don't look back." Antxon was moving so fast I knew if I took my eyes off him for a minute I would lose him. We were coming up to the Tenth mile. I could see the water. My legs were getting tired. They were hurting around the ankles, and the arch of my feet. I wasn't short of breath yet but at our pace it would not be too far behind. When we hit the tenth mile, Antxon picked up his pace again. I want to say that we were sprinting at this point, we had over three miles to go and I was not even close to giving up or slowing down.

It reminded me of running in Costa Rica. How I ran to the top of the mountain in Escazu.

At the top of the mountain, I found a great restaurant called Mirador Tiquicia. On a clear day it had such a great view. I would stand there a minute and look at the amazing view.

I think you are able to see all of San Jose from there. Then I would sprint down the mountain as fast as I could all the way down past highway 27. I would go under the bridge and head towards Santana.

It definitely felt familiar; I felt like I was back in Escazu. I heard someone call out to me and for a moment I thought it was Myra. I had not heard that voice in a while but I didn't want to turn around. She called out to me again and I glanced over to the left, it was Tatiana, a friend of mine. Gosh, I have not talked to or seen her in years. I looked forward to keeping my attention on Antxon and he was gone. Just like that I was running faster than ever looking for Antxon and wondering how I was going to find him.

Tatiana ran towards me and we ran together for the next two miles. I had forgotten how fast she was, and that she had a ton of experience running in marathons.

By the time we got to the twelve mile, Zelia called out to us. She said, “Where is Antxon?”

I said, “I’m not sure. I lost him about two miles ago.” She pointed to the left and Antxon was waiting for us on the side of the road. Antxon yelled out to follow him. He said, “Myra is just behind us.”

The pace was so fast my lungs started to burn along with my legs. I felt like a plane looking for a good place to crash. Whenever you entertain the thought of pain it never goes well. I could finally see the finish line. My heart was pounding trying to keep up with Antxon and Zelia. Tatiana knew Myra, she ran with her several times. Tatiana started yelling, “Come on, guys, you have to do better than that, Myra is not playing.”

I took large strides and placed my hands down by my side, and took a few huge breaths, and I focused on nothing but the finish line. I didn’t know how close Myra was so I leaned forward as I crossed the finish line. I could hardly hear anyone talking, my ear buds were soaking wet and my eyes were filled with sweat. I walked over to the recovery station with Antxon and Zelia. I just needed a minute to pull myself together.

I grabbed a drink and some food. I sat down on the ground leaning up against a fence.

I was thinking about my life and my bucket list. I was thinking about my friends and the direction I was going with my life. I finally realized that, “If you don’t make the time to work on creating the life you want, you’re eventually going to be forced to spend a lot of time dealing with a life you don’t want.” So get busy, and start living the life you want to live.

The choice is ultimately up to you.

Bibliography

Andrews, E. (2017 January 17) The Treacherous Race to the South Pole. Retrieved from: https://www.history.com/news/the-treacherous-race-to-the-south-pole

Arc, J. (2021 May 26) St. Joan of Arc, Written by: Malcolm G.A. Vale, Yvonne Lanhers. Retrieved from: https://www.britannica.com/biography/Saint-Joan-of-Arc

Coats, C (2019, February 7) Forbes: How to Decide Whether You're Ready for a Coach. Retrieved from: https://www.forbes.com/sites/forbescoachescouncil/2019/02/07/how-to-decide-whether-youre-ready-for-a-coach/?sh=a345e911915a

Odin, L (2017, June 11) Sports Retriever: They do What? 30 athletes and their rituals. Retrieved from: https://www.sportsretriever.com/uncategorized/30-athletes-rituals/

Becker, K (2008, October 28) Runner's World Magazine: Running Shoes FAQ. https://www.runnersworld.com/gear/a20806543/running-shoe-questions

Kennedy, J (2019, December 14) Blog: Why Pope Julius may be the most important pope in history. https://vaticantips.com/pope-julius-ii/

Taylor, J. Ph.D (2009, October 30) Psychology Today, Sports: What Motivates Athletes? How Athletes Maximize their Motivation. Retrieved from: https://www.psychologytoday.com/us/blog/the-power-prime/200910/sports-what-motivates-athletes

Weihenmayer, E. (2021, July 1) Overingcomming Fear, It's the first step in becoming the best we can be-in life, in business, in relationships. Live a no barriers life. Retrieved from: https://erikweihenmayer.com/

Women's Museum of California, (2019, March 13) Breaking Through the Fog-The Career of Florence Chadwick. Retrieved from: https://womensmuseum.wordpress.com/2019/03/13/breaking-through-the-fog-the-career-of-florence-chadwick/

Xavier, V. (2017, May 26) Quora, What are some unknown facts about the Sistine Chapel. Retrieved From: https://www.quora.com/What-are-some-unknown-facts-about-the-Sistine-Chapel

Ngo, K. Goodreads.com, Quotes from Kevin Ngo. https://www.goodreads.com/author/quotes/6548267.Kevin_Ngo

About the Author

Will Cramer is the author of The Mighty Marathon. He enjoys running in different parts of the country. He runs half-marathons, Spartan obstacles races and enjoys running in other countries. Will has a B.S from Liberty University in Business Administration and a Masters in Education from East Stroudsburg University. Will has been teaching students with disabilities for the past 18 years.

www.ingramcontent.com/pod-product-compliance
Lightning Source LLC
La Vergne TN
LVHW010459160826
845677LV00012B/2559